THINGS FOR JESUS TO DO

BY CONSTANCE MURRAY

RoseDog Books

PITTSBURGH, PENNSYLVANIA 15238

RoseDog Books
585 Alpha Drive
Suite 103
Pittsburgh, PA 15238
Visit our website at *www.rosedogbookstore.com*

ISBN: 978-1-64957-845-7
eISBN: 978-1-64957-865-5

THINGS FOR JESUS TO DO

I dedicated my book Things for Jesus to Do to my Lord and Savior to Jesus Christ for making me a beautiful woman of God in spirit of my trial and tribulation. To my family which lived inside of me Harriet Tubman my grandmother Hattie Davis my mother Mary Shirley Chisolm Barbara Walter Maya Angela these are my angels of life. I would like to thank my wonderful son. My two love heart Sean and Delanno who gave a listned ear o my books beleive in my effort as a mother and writer.

The idea of Things for Jesue to Do was drop like a teardrop from heaven on my face after crying one morning after I awaken I got a called asking for me to pray for them then it occur to me all the thing which we ask Jesue to do for us that whys I wrote this book I hope it will filled your heart with new things and open your eye and let you know God is always listening to your prayer let God be the glory in your life no matter what.

I love you as long as you keep reading my books I will keep writing them always

Constance Murray

Dedication Page

I would like to thank wonderful staff at Dorrance Publishing first most Mr Andrew Rouce saying go ahead you can write it Constance encourge word helping me beleive in myself who always listned to my idea on my future book and especially to Ms Ashley Austgen project service manager

PRAY
FOR
MOTHER

PRAY
FOR
FATHER

PRAY

FOR

SISTER

PRAY

FOR

BROTHER

PRAY

FOR

GRANDMOTHER

PRAY
FOR
GRANDFATHER

PRAY

FOR

AUNT

PRAY

FOR

STOP

SEX

TRAFFIC

PRAY

FOR

ALEX

Pray

to Stop

Fire

in

California

PRAY

FOR

STOP

GLOBE

WARMING

Pray

For

Cure

Mental

Health

PRAY
FOR
CURE
BLINDNESS

PRAY

FOR

NEW

KIDNEY

PRAY
FOR
HOMELESS
CURE

PRAY

FOR

LOVE

PRAY

FOR

MY

UNCLE

PRAY

FOR

COUSIN

PRAY

FOR

WISDOM

Pray

For

Shoes

PRAY
FOR
RAIN

PRAY

FOR

WHALES

PRAY

FOR

JUDGES

PRAY
FOR
COAT

PRAY

FOR

PEACE

PRAY
FOR
DONALD

PRAY
FOR
HAPPY

PRAY

FOR

PASTOR

PRAY
FOR
FIRST
LADY

PRAY

FOR

JOBS

PRAY

FOR

COOKIE

Pray

For

Cancer

Cure

Pray

For

Heart

PRAY

FOR

KIDNEY

PRAY FOR PRISON

PRAY
FOR
PARIS

PRAY
FOR
WASHINGTON DC

Pray

For

College

PRAY

FOR

NEW

YEAR

2020

PRAY

VIOLENCE

STOP

PRAY
FOR
MILITARY

PRAY
FOR
CHINA

PRAY

FOR

WATER

PRAY

FOR

AFRICA

PRAY
FOR
NEW ZEALAND

PRAY
FOR
GREENLAND

Pray

To

Become

Lawyer

PRAY

TO

BECOME

WRITER

PRAY
FOR
HUMANITY

PRAY

I

GRADUATED

FROM

SCHOOL

PRAY
FOR
TEDDY BEAR

PRAY

FOR

HOSPITAL

PRAY
FOR
SUPER
BOWL

PRAY
FOR
TEACHER

PRAY

FOR

SPACE

PROGRAM

PRAY

FOR

GEORGIA

PRAY
FOR
MICHIGAN

PRAY
FOR
CHICAGO

PRAY
FOR
LOVE

PRAY
FOR
SNOW

PRAY
FOR
FOOD

PRAY

FOR

VETERAN

Pray
For
Money

PRAY

FOR

LAWYER

PRAY
FOR
CLOTHES

PRAY

FOR

PHONE

PRAY

FOR

CHURCH

PRAY
FOR
MY DOG

PRAY FOR MY CAT

Pray
For
Bob

PRAY
FOR
SUSAN

PRAY

FOR

HOUSE

PRAY
FOR
NEW
GLASS

PRAY
FOR
RAIN

PRAY
TO
LOSE
WEIGHT

PRAY

FOR

A

CURE

DEMENTIA

PRAY
FOR
CURE
MULTIPLE
SCLEROSIS

PRAY
FOR
CURE
BLINDNESS

PRAY

FOR

CURE

EPILEPSY

PRAY
I
WIN
AT
OSCAR

PRAY

FOR

CLEAN

WATER

THANK

YOU

FOR

LOVE

THANK YOU FOR MY COWBOY HAT

THANK
YOU
FOR
BICYCLE

PRAY
FOR
PRESIDENT

PRAY

STOP

FORCLOSURE

PRAY

TO

BECOME

ARTIST

Pray
For
Rainforest

PRAY

TO SAVE

ELEPHANT

PRAY
TO
STOP
BANKRUPTCY

PRAY

TO

BECOME

NEUROLOGIST

PRAY
TO
BECOME
SCIENTIST

PRAYING

FOR

HEARING

AID

PRAY
TO
BECOME
SINGER

PRAY
FOR
PROTECTION

Pray

I

Finish

School

PRAY

TO

BECOME

PLUMBER

Pray

To

Become

Engineer

PRAY

TO

BECOME

VETERINARIAN